NATURAL RESOURCES

NANCY DICKMANN

T0014659

BROWN BEAR BOOKS

Published by Brown Bear Books Ltd

4877 N. Circulo Bujia
Tucson, AZ 85718
USA

and

Studio G14, Regent Studios,
1 Thane Villas, London N7 7PH, UK

ISBN 978-1-78121-816-7 (library bound)
ISBN 978-1-78121-822-8 (paperback)

Library of Congress Cataloging-in-Publication Data available on request

Design: squareandcircus.co.uk
Design Manager: Keith Davis
Children's Publisher: Anne O'Daly

Manufactured in the United States of America
CPSIA compliance information: Batch#AG/5652

Picture Credits

The photographs in this book are used by permission and through the courtesy of:

iStock: fstop123 16–17; Shutterstock: muratart 14–15, naramit 18–19, H M Shahidul Islam 6–7, sjgh 10–11, TippaPatt 20–21, WitR 4–5, Lexter Yap 8–9, Larina Yulia 12–13.

All other artwork and photography © Brown Bear Books.

t-top, r-right, l-left, c-center, b-bottom

Brown Bear Books has made every attempt to contact the copyright holder. If you have any information about omissions, please contact: licensing@brownbearbooks.co.uk

Websites

The website addresses in this book were valid at the time of going to press. However, it is possible that contents or addresses may change following publication of this book.
No responsibility for any such changes can be accepted by the author or the publisher. Readers should be supervised when they access the Internet.

Words in **bold** appear in the Glossary on page 23.

CONTENTS

EARTH'S RESOURCES

Earth is our home. And it has everything we need! Natural resources are things that are found in nature. People can use them. Stone, wood, and air are all natural resources. We depend on them.

RENEWABLE RESOURCES

Some resources are **renewable**. They will not run out. Sunlight is renewable. So is wood. We plant new trees to replace the ones we cut down. Other resources are not renewable. Once we have used up Earth's supply, there will be no more. Metals are not renewable.

Humans have always used natural resources. The Egyptian pyramids are made of stone.

Natural Resources at Home

We use natural resources every day.

We use water for washing.

Sheets are made from cotton. This is a plant.

A lot of our electricity comes from burning fuels.

Food cans are made from metal. So are frying pans.

Some furniture is made of wood.

We eat plants such as fruits, vegetables, and grains.

Televisions have metals and glass. Glass is made from sand.

WATER

What makes our planet special? Water! Nearly three-quarters of Earth's surface is covered in water. Most of it is in the oceans. This water is a habitat for sea creatures. But it is too salty for us to use.

FRESHWATER

Only three percent of water is **freshwater**. It flows in rivers and lakes. Some of it is ice. Ice forms glaciers and ice caps. We use freshwater for drinking, washing, and cooking. We use it for watering **crops**. We even use flowing water to make **electricity**!

Not everyone has access to clean water. It is a precious resource. We shouldn't waste it.

Dinosaur Drinks

Earth's water has been around for a long time. It is still the same water as it was billions of years ago. Maybe the water you drink was once drunk by a dinosaur!

The Water Cycle

Earth's freshwater gets **recycled**. This is called the water cycle.

3. It cools down and forms clouds.

4. Water falls as rain or snow.

2. The gas is water vapor. It rises into the sky.

1. Water **evaporates** from oceans and lakes. It turns into a gas.

5. It soaks into the ground. It collects in rivers and streams.

6. Water flows back into the oceans.

SUN AND AIR

You would only last a few minutes without air. Divers carry air in tanks.

We couldn't live without the Sun. We use its heat and light every day. Its **energy** helps crops grow. We use it to make electricity. Without the Sun, Earth would freeze. There would be no clouds and wind. There would be no light or life.

THE AIR

Clean air is also a natural resource. Animals need its **oxygen** to breathe. So do humans. Moving air is called wind. It has movement energy. Wind **turbines** turn this energy into electricity.

The Oxygen Cycle

Oxygen is one gas in the air.
Carbon dioxide is another.

Plants take in carbon dioxide from the air. Using sunlight, they turn it into food.

Plants release oxygen. It goes into the air.

Dead living things rot away. This releases carbon dioxide.

Fuels need oxygen to burn. The burning releases carbon dioxide.

Animals and humans breathe in oxygen. We breathe out carbon dioxide.

ROCKS AND MINERALS

Earth is a ball of rock. Its rocks are made up of **minerals**. They come in different types. Some rocks are hard and sharp. Others are soft and crumbly. Many of them are useful. The lead in your pencil is a type of mineral. So is the talc in baby powder.

USING ROCKS

Early humans made stone tools. They chipped flakes away to leave sharp edges. Later, people built homes from stones. The Ancient Romans built bridges and roads. They used rocks to make concrete for buildings.

Glass is made from sand. Most sand is made of tiny pieces of rock. When it's heated, they melt.

Rocks and Minerals Everywhere

Today, we use rocks and minerals in many different ways.

Glass for mirrors and jars.

Stones for walls and houses.

Chalk for writing and drawing.

Gravel as a base for railroad tracks.

Making concrete and cement.

Marble for sculptures.

Granite for kitchen countertops.

Salt for flavoring food.

METALS

Metals are natural substances. We usually find them in rocks. Metals are often shiny. They can be hammered into shape. Most metals are hard and strong. Many are good at passing on heat or electricity.

USING METALS

Metals are everywhere! People wear gold and silver jewelry. Copper wires carry electricity. We drink from aluminum cans. We store food in steel ones. Steel is very strong. It is used in buildings. Cars and trucks are made of steel.

Metals melt when they are heated. They are poured into molds. Then they cool and harden.

7. The recycled aluminum is cooled into a block.

1. A can starts as a block of aluminum.

2. Heavy rollers press it into a flat sheet.

6. The cans are shredded and melted down.

Reusing Metals

Many drinks come in aluminum cans. This metal can be recycled. It is used over and over.

3. The sheet is cut and formed into cans.

5. Used cans are collected. They are cleaned and crushed.

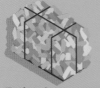

4. The cans are filled and sold.

FUELS

An airplane has powerful engines. They burn a fuel called kerosene.

In our daily lives, we depend on energy. We use heat to cook food. We use it to keep our homes warm. We use electricity to power gadgets. We use engines in vehicles and machines. All of these uses need fuel.

RELEASING ENERGY

A fuel is a natural substance. It contains a lot of stored energy. Burning a fuel releases that energy. Fuels give off heat when they burn. The heat can run a **power plant**. It can power an engine. It can toast a marshmallow.

Running Out

Wood is a renewable resource. We can always grow more trees. But we can't grow oil or coal. We are using up Earth's supply. Once it's gone, there will be no more.

Types of Fuel

We use many different kinds of fuel.

Wood comes from trees.

Natural gas is found underground.

Coal is a rock found underground.

Oil is a thick liquid. It is made into gasoline and other fuels.

Some people burn dried animal poop for cooking.

Biodiesel comes from soybeans and other plants.

WOOD

Wood is an important fuel. But it has many other uses. Wood is strong but fairly light. It is easy to saw into shape. Best of all, wood is renewable. We cut down trees to use their wood. But we can plant new trees to replace them.

WOOD EVERYWHERE

We build fences out of wood. Tall wooden poles carry power cables and phone lines. Furniture and floorboards are made of wood. We use bark chips in gardens. We even stir our pots with wooden spoons!

Many houses have a strong wooden frame. It supports the walls and roof.

Trees are Terrific!

Trees give us wood. They provide shade. Some trees produce fruits and nuts. Trees also make oxygen. We need it to breathe. Without trees, we couldn't survive!

Making Paper

A lot of paper comes from pine trees. It often has recycled paper mixed in.

The wood is cut into small chips.

The chips are mixed with steam and chemicals.

The mixture breaks down into a soggy pulp.

The pulp is sprayed onto a wire screen.

The damp pulp is fed through heated rollers. They press and dry it.

The paper goes onto huge rolls. It's ready to use.

SOIL

Take a look down at the ground. Can you see soil? Soil is like a living skin covering Earth's rock. It is an important resource. Without it, crops could not grow. Soil also helps recycle air and water.

PROTECTING SOIL

Soil takes a very long time to form. We must protect what we have. Soil can dry out and blow away. It can also be washed away by water. This is called erosion. Soil can be damaged by harmful chemicals. This is called pollution.

Thanks to Worms

Worms help keep soil healthy. They eat dead plants and animals. They poop out their **nutrients**. It's like recycling! Worms also loosen and mix soil as they move.

Rich soil is full of nutrients. Plants need these to grow.

What Soil is Made Of

Soil is a mixture of five main ingredients.

Air This leaves hollow spaces so water can drain through.

Rocks and minerals These are in tiny pieces. Most are no bigger than a grain of sand.

Living things Bacteria and fungi are just two examples.

Water Plants can suck this up through their roots.

Organic matter This is the remains of dead plants and animals. It's broken down into tiny pieces.

19

FOOD

Food is one of the most important natural resources. Without it, we wouldn't last long! All of our food starts with plants. We eat many plants as they are. Bananas and apples are a good example. We turn other plants, like wheat, into different products.

WHAT ABOUT MEAT?

Even meat starts with a plant! Most farm animals eat plants. Their bodies take in the energy in plants. They use it to grow. When we eat those animals, the energy passes to us.

Bees and other insects carry pollen from flower to flower. This helps plants make seeds.

Key Crops

These plants are some of the world's most important crops. Millions of people depend on them.

Corn is good to eat. It is also used to feed animals. We can make fuel from corn.

Wheat is often made into flour. We use it in bread, bagels, and tortillas.

Rice is an important grain. It comes in different varieties.

Potatoes grow underground. We can bake, fry, or boil them.

Soybeans have a lot of uses. We make them into tofu and soy milk. Their oil is used for cooking.

QUIZ

How much have you learned about natural resources? It's time to test your knowledge!

1. About how much of Earth's surface is covered in water?
a. one quarter
b. half
c. three quarters

2. What is glass made from?
a. sand
b. water
c. plastic

3. How do we release the energy stored in a fuel?
a. by chopping it up
b. by burning it
c. by soaking it in water

4. Which of these is not an ingredient in soil?
a. tiny pieces of rock
b. dead living things
c. helium

The answers are on page 24.

GLOSSARY

crop a type of plant grown as food or for other uses

electricity a form of energy that flows as a current, which we can use to power devices

energy the ability to do work

evaporate to turn from a liquid into a gas

freshwater water that does not have salt dissolved in it

mineral a non-living natural substance that forms a structure with a repeating pattern

nutrients natural substances that help living things grow and thrive

oxygen a gas in the air that humans and animals need to breathe

recycle to take waste materials and reuse them by turning their materials into new objects

renewable able to be replaced instead of running out

power plant a factory where other forms of energy are turned into electricity

turbine a large fan-like machine that spins when air or water flows past its blades

FIND OUT MORE

Books

How We Use Wood. Nancy Dickmann, Crabtree Publishing, 2020.

Natural Resources (Ecographics). Izzi Howell, Franklin Watts, 2019.

Natural Resources (Flowchart Smart). Richard and Louise Spilsbury, Gareth Stevens Publishing, 2019.

Websites

bbc.co.uk/bitesize/topics/zshp34j/articles/z62qy9q

dkfindout.com/uk/science/materials/metals/

kids.britannica.com/kids/article/natural-resource/399553

INDEX

Answers: 1. c; 2. a; 3. b; 4. c